The World's Worst Diabetes Mom

REAL-LIFE STORIES OF PARENTING
A CHILD WITH TYPE 1 DIABETES

Stacey Simms

SPARK Publications

Charlotte, North Carolina

The World's Worst Diabetes Mom:
Real-Life Stories of Parenting a Child with Type 1 Diabetes
Stacey Simms

Designed, produced, and published by SPARK Publications, SPARKpublications.com
Charlotte, North Carolina

Printed in the United States of America.
Softcover, October 2019, ISBN: 978-1-943070-66-4
E-book, October 2019, ISBN: 978-1-943070-67-1
Library of Congress Control Number: 2019910981

Dedication

For my mother, Arlene Simms, who never demanded perfection, but who always made sure I was safe and happy. I guess that makes you "worst" first.

For Slade, Lea, and Benny who fill my heart with laughter and love.

Medical Disclaimer

The information contained in this book is not
intended as medical advice and is not a substitute
for the services of and information from a
trained health care provider.

Table of Contents

Introduction

This isn't the book I set out to write. The original idea was to put together a bunch of my old blog posts, add some updated information, and send it out into the world. But I found myself adding and rewriting and being frustrated with "just" the information. I've been a diabetes parent for more than 12 years. What did I really want to say?

Information is available in many places. You can Google any question you have right now. And a bunch of wonderful, informative diabetes books are already on the market. But I wanted to get to the bottom of what I'd learned after more than a decade of raising a child with type 1 diabetes (T1D) and more than four years hosting "Diabetes Connections," a podcast about T1D. How could I really add to the conversation and help?

Then someone on Facebook told me I was an awful parent.

Perfection has never sat well with me. It's also never sat close to me. With or without diabetes. My philosophy (and you'll hear it a lot in these pages) is "not perfect, but safe and happy." I was called out on that by another parent who vehemently disagreed. It got ugly, as can happen on social media, and I decided to back off. I gave up arguing and wrote, "I guess I'm the world's worst diabetes mom." That's when the lightbulb went on.

Our son was diagnosed in 2006, just before he turned 2 years old. Our diabetes philosophy has always been about acknowledging the bad and being realistic about how diabetes can mess things up and slow us down. We're not a "T1D will never stop us" kind of family. Diabetes stinks. It *can* stop you. But then you correct or treat or whatever you need to do to keep going and help your child live the life he or she wants. You cry, you laugh, and you keep moving forward.

Our endocrinologist, Dr. V, gave us a gift the first day we met him. In addition to getting down on the floor and playing with my son, Benny (and answering all of my questions – I basically gave him the equivalent of a job interview), he said that we needed to realize that a lot of treating and managing diabetes was as much of an art as a science. Over the next few months as we learned how to take care of Benny, Dr. V would help us see that numbers, while extremely important, weren't always exact and shouldn't be allowed to run our lives. He wanted Benny to grow up as a person with diabetes, not as a person defined by diabetes.

We needed to remember, always, that we were raising a child. Not a number, not a graph, not a lab result. Benny would always be more than his A1C or his time in range.

When I found the diabetes online community a few years later, I found not everyone was as lucky to have had that guidance early on. It also seemed like the worry about numbers, the search for exact measurements, and the pursuit of perfection were cropping up more and more. Since Benny's diagnosis in 2006, I've felt a shift from people talking and sharing about living well with type 1 diabetes to living perfectly with it.

Was this part of the trend in parenting where we all felt like we must be perfect to be successful and raise good kids? Is it unique to diabetes where we really do feel like we're graded on our actions? I mean, there are numbers every single day and, now with continuous glucose monitoring, every single minute. It's almost impossible to not correlate a feeling to those numbers.

I realized pretty quickly that I can't play that game. Perfection is not in my parenting wheelhouse. In fact, I welcome mistakes. It's how I learn. I improve by getting it wrong the first time around. I'd argue that mistakes make us all better.

Maybe you're just starting out with a newly diagnosed child. If so, I hope this book can guide you through some basic concepts and help you recognize that, while you will make mistakes, your child with diabetes can be safe and happy. If you've been in the

"Build a successful team (and company) utilizing this book. Amanda and Brenda have broken down an overwhelming process into clear steps anyone can follow to hire better candidates in a shorter amount of time."

–**Justin Donald**, Investor, Entrepreneur, Podcast Host, and Author of the #1 *WSJ* and *USA Today* Bestseller, *The Lifestyle Investor*

"You will hire someone, but will you hire the right person on purpose? In a world of vague outlines and fingers-crossed attempts, this book provides clarity and intentionality. The Hiring Process is a natural outpouring of Brenda and Amanda's attention to detail and relationship-first mindset."

–**Mike Domeny**, speaker, actor, and author of *Thrown off Script: Turn Interruptions into Opportunities and Thrive in the Unexpected*

"The strategy and tools provided in this book will benefit entrepreneurs and HR teams of all sizes. The Hiring Process is a wise investment for any business owner looking to simplify and save time and resources."

–**Dexter Godfrey**, Founder and CEO of Leadership and Sales Academy

"In the lifecycle of a business, there comes a point where the *grand experiment* becomes a profitable venture. Once this happens, the business owner quickly realizes the business has grown beyond them. In order to scale, they need a team to help them carry the vision. This is a make-or-break point in most businesses, and it depends on two factors: (1) the business leader's growth mindset, and (2) a systemized process for hiring that ensures the right team is in place to scale the business. This book provides the tools to make bridging this critical gap an easier step to the next level in business."

–**Brenda Dunagan**, CEO Dunagan and Associates LLC

THE HIRING PROCESS

A COMPLETE SYSTEM TO **SAVE TIME, SIMPLIFY STEPS,** AND **STRENGTHEN YOUR TEAM**

Other Books by the Authors

The Team Solution Series

The Author Solution Series

Also by Brenda A. Haire

TheJoyOfPursuit.com

THE
HIRING
PROCESS

A COMPLETE SYSTEM TO
SAVE TIME, SIMPLIFY STEPS,
AND **STRENGTHEN YOUR TEAM**

AMANDA J. PAINTER
and
BRENDA A. HAIRE

BOOK 1
THE TEAM SOLUTION SERIES

Published by Joy of Pursuit Publishing

Chandler, Texas 75758

JoyOfPursuitPublishing.com

Library of Congress Cataloging: 2021924011

Softcover: 978-1-957205-00-7

Hardcover: 978-1-957205-01-4

E-book: 978-1-957205-02-1

Throughout the book you'll be introduced to new tools. We provide examples, templates, checklists, email copy, and more.

Download your free bundle at
theJoyOfPursuit.com/Hiring

@JoyofPursuit

Dedication

We dedicate this book to all the overwhelmed business owners and their teams giving their best effort and building companies that change lives.

Contents

Contents

Foreword

Does anyone enjoy the daunting task of hiring—or as Amanda and Brenda put it—"solving company issues?" I sure don't. Not every issue is solved by creating a role and hiring someone new, but getting the right people in the right positions is the most important thing a company can do for culture, growth, and fulfillment of purpose. Finding the right *who* for any position can be difficult but is vital for forward progress.

Amanda and Brenda have remarkable gifts and abilities to see the big picture and then organize and implement a strategic plan to get there. Having worked with them firsthand through a course creation and collaboration, I'm not surprised that the two of them have written such a clear guide to help any small business through the hiring process.

The Hiring Process is a step-by-step guide from start to finish. From creating the job description to writing the rejection letter, they've got you covered. Plus, they provide templates, checklists, worksheets, email samples, and explanations. It's not enough to know you need this system, but knowing *why* you need it and *how* it will serve you and your team in the long run is valuable in and of itself.

This quick read will save you time, energy, resources, and capital. As a small business owner, you should be jumping for joy that these two finally provided the world a resource so simple, yet elaborate, that will guide you not once but again and again through the lifetime of your company. Wow, what a great investment this book is for your company and future! Great job, Brenda and Amanda, and thanks for giving business owners a resource that will bring joy amidst a detailed and critical process.

Tyler Wagner, Founder of Authors Unite | *WSJ* Bestselling Author

A Note to You—the Reader

At most companies, people spend 2% of their time recruiting and 75% managing their recruiting mistakes.

—Richard Fairbank

The success of all organizations is dependent on its people. For this reason, the hiring process is vital to business success and worth the time and energy to develop. A structured approach to recruitment is necessary for optimization, and consistency in all stages will yield informed hiring decisions. Once developed and implemented, this system will save you time and resources and help you achieve long-term employment success.

The key to successfully hiring the right individuals is in following these important steps in the hiring process:

- determine your needs and resources
- collaborate with your team
- communicate clearly and effectively
- utilize tools for efficiency
- analyze the data
- evaluate based on objective criteria
- reduce time spent in interviews

The success of all organizations is dependent on its people.

Of the above actions, *communication* is the most essential. Keeping communication front of mind during hiring will result in a people-focused mindset instead of a fill-the-vacancy mindset. As you read, you will learn how good communication is key in every step of the hiring process.

Furthermore, this book will help you and your team understand and define your various needs and roles. It will in turn allow potential candidates to better understand the position in consideration. Accurately defining the position will contribute to employee satisfaction and therefore employee retention.

For consistency, this book will use the sample position of "Strategic Assistant" throughout. While there are unlimited options for examples, we feel that the Strategic Assistant is relevant to most hiring situations. Whether your small business has one or one hundred employees, it is likely that someone or some department in your company needs a Strategic Assistant.

So, if you're ready to implement a clear hiring system, the book you are holding will be your guide along the way.

Chapter One

Team-Based Approach

*Unity is strength ... when there
is teamwork and collaboration,
wonderful things can be achieved.*

—Mattie Stepanek

When expanding your personnel, don't neglect the input and usefulness of your current staff. Use a team-based approach to growing. If you are currently a solopreneur, you can enlist the help of a trusted friend or board member or hire a consultant to guide you.

Hiring should be a collaborative effort. The simple methodology shared in this book will allow for more input from others in your company. Different personalities will naturally take to different elements in the process to make for a more balanced hiring decision. Don't get overwhelmed as you read through the tasks ahead. If you have a team, we will show you the best ways to utilize them in this process to free you from the detailed work involved.

When collaborating with your team about the open position and the hiring process, here's a

Make hiring a collaborative effort.

word of caution: Don't allow overwhelmed or overworked team members who need help in their department to hire out of desperation. Be sure to have unbiased team members weigh in with an outside perspective. It's too easy for someone who is drowning to grab the life vest of whoever shows up rather than being patient in the process and selecting the best candidate for the long term.

Team Capacity Check

When you are ready to hire, the first step is to check in with your current team. We recommend doing this annually, regardless of your hiring plans. You may just find the perfect fit for the new position inside the company.

Three Reasons to Conduct a Capacity Check Prior to an External Hire:

You may

1. uncover someone's desire to take on more work.
2. discover someone with skills or experience in the area of need.
3. realize a team member's desire to grow into a new position.

Suggested Capacity Check Questions that Relate to the Hiring Process:

> Are you satisfied with your current workload? Or do you have the capacity and desire for more?

> Do you have a skill set that isn't being utilized? If so, what are these skills?

See a full list of Team Capacity Check questions at the end of this chapter.

With these findings, you may realize that you don't need to hire another team member yet. Or you may discover that you have someone willing to pick up the extra work until the new team member is in place.

When considering a current team member for additional responsibilities or a new role, do not entrust these duties without fully vetting them through the process mapped out in the rest of this book. It may appear easier to utilize a current team member instead of looking outside of your business, but if the person is not truly fit for the job, it will cost you, your team, and your business more time and resources in the long run.

Team Capacity Check

1. What job role, duties, or day-to-day items do you find irritating?
2. What job role, duties, or day-to-day items do you find to just be OK?
3. What job role, duties, or day-to-day items do you find fascinating and motivating?
4. Do you find your workload reasonable?
5. Are you satisfied with your current workload? Or have the capacity and desire for more hours or projects?
6. Do you believe work is distributed evenly across your team?
7. How would you rate the way our organization makes use of your strengths?
8. Do you have a skill set that isn't being utilized? If so, what?
9. Is there an area of the company that you are interested in learning more about?
10. Are your responsibilities clear to you and those you work with?
11. Do you have access to everything you need to perform to the best of your ability?
12. Do you have the appropriate amount of information to make correct decisions about your work including feedback?
13. How would you rate communication in our organization?
14. Do you feel that you are growing professionally?
15. Do you feel that your job allows you to develop new skills?
16. Do you see a path to advance your career in our company?
17. Which Core Value do you relate to most and why?
18. What do you want to be remembered for?
19. In what ways do you like to be recognized? Financially, public praise, gifts, rewards, special activities?
20. Do you have any other input, suggestions, or ideas you'd like to share with the Leadership Team?

Chapter Two

Creating a Job Description

*True leadership isn't about having an idea.
It's about having an idea and recruiting other
people to execute on this vision.*

—Leila Janah

Team communication begins *before* you hire. A well-thought-out Job Description is the first step of this communication. You cannot assume expectations will be met if they are not properly communicated. The Job Description will lay the groundwork for these expectations and set the new team member up for success, which will in turn aid in the success of your business.

Accuracy in the Job Description contributes to employee retention, saving you valuable resources.

Determine Your Needs and Define a Goal

Start with the problem you are trying to solve. Some examples include the following:

- I get too many useless emails.
- This (identify task) pulls me away from my most important work.
- Things (identify) are slipping through the cracks.
- We get too many customer complaints. (What is the common theme of these complaints?)
- We can't seem to get any leads.

Now that you've identified the issue, define the solution.

I need someone to:

- provide quality control
- create and implement organizational processes
- reduce the tech team's workload
- expand our social media outreach
- research and recommend more efficient software

While you're still early in the process, collaborate with your team. Remember, this is also the candidate's *future* team. Do they agree with the hiring objective? Is this issue and solution appropriate? Is hiring the next best step for the team? Providing the opportunity to give feedback and create buy-in is essential for a healthy team dynamic. Team members feel valued when they are involved in the decision-making. Moving ahead without full participation from the relevant team members will damage morale and ultimately affect the company's bottom line.

Who on your team should you collaborate with? Here are some potential individuals and departments to consider:

- Human Resources
- Finance
- Technology
- Executive(s)
- Manager of open position
- Employees who perform in a similar role
- Employees who will interact with this hire regularly

If you are a solopreneur, we urge you not to carry this burden alone. You can ask a trusted friend who knows your business or reach out to us for a consultation.

Once you establish a goal, envision how the position will fit into the overall picture of the company. Any new hire will impact the rest of your team. Pause and ask these questions:

- Who will the new hire report to directly?
- What key employees or teams will they interact with the most?
- Where does this role sit on the team's organizational chart?
- Does this role qualify as an employee, or is it contractor work?

It's important to understand worker classifications and know that legal repercussions may result if hired incorrectly. An independent contractor works for themselves, completing work for another business based on contracted deliverables. Independent contractors are responsible to pay all taxes on their earnings. Whereas an employee performs work that is under direct control of the employer, and the work is integral to the operations of the business. Employee wages are subject to tax withholdings and employer-paid payroll taxes.

In the U.S., three categories must be considered when determining worker status: Behavior Control, Financial Control, and Relationship. The following list highlights the key points, but it is not a fully inclusive list of all items to be evaluated:

Behavior Control

- When—Is there a requirement of set hours? Or does the worker have the autonomy to choose when to work?
- Where—Is work required at the employer's place of business?
- How—Are specific instructions provided on how to perform the work? Or is it at the discretion of the worker?

Financial Control

- Frequency of payment—Are they paid hourly, weekly, monthly, commission, or is pay directly tied to project completion?
- Significant investment—Which party makes the investment in tools, equipment, and training? Are they employer-provided, or does the worker use their own?

Relationship

- Employee-type benefits—Does the worker have benefits such as paid time off or health insurance?
- Permanency of work—Is the work ongoing, timeframe-specific, or project-based?

For more information, visit IRS.gov, review labor laws for your state, and discuss with your tax professional.

Now that you are clear about whether you seek to hire a contractor or an employee, specify other key features of the role. You will list these at the beginning of the Job Description. Assess what is necessary to communicate first and what a candidate would need to consider when applying for your position.

- Location: In office, remote, or hybrid?
- Is it an entry-, mid-, or executive-level position?
- Full time, part time, or contractor?
- Salaried or hourly?

When titling the position, use a title that does not diminish the role, responsibility, or the individual accepting the position. If the team member will manage processes, use a title such as manager, coordinator, or director. If the team member will lead others, use a title such as director, lead, or chief if they sit in the c-suite or leadership team. If the team member will assist others, the title of assistant is fine but don't use it flippantly. You want to give titles that edify—titles your team will be proud to display beside their names.

If it fits with your company culture, use creative titles, such as Chief of Happiness for

Use a title that does not diminish the role, responsibility, or the individual accepting the position.

your customer service lead. Don't feel like you need to force a creative title, but be mindful of the words you use to describe someone's role in your company.

Job Description Outline

About Your Company

Inform job seekers about more than just the job—provide important details about your company too. A Job Description is essentially an advertisement to work at your company. This is your opportunity to sell the ideals of your company and share why someone would want to work for you. Keep it brief, though; a few sentences or bullet points will do. This portion of the Job Description is used to share a broad view of the company. An applicant who wants to learn more can do so by visiting your website.

Suggestions:

- How is your company unique?
- What are your company's values?
- What is your Vision Purpose Statement?
- Have you received any relevant awards, e.g., Best Workplace or Best in the Industry?
- Are you an entrepreneurial startup or a family-owned business founded over a century ago?

Including this information on a Job Description will help the potential applicant understand your vision and company culture. This can either deter an applicant if they do not share similar values or motivate an applicant who shares your values and wants to work with others of a similar mindset. (We will later teach you how to utilize this as a tool in the interview process.)

Success

Wrap up the more descriptive portion of the Job Description with two to three clear statements of what it takes to be successful in the role.

- Who is the ideal candidate?
- What does success look like?
- How is it measured?

This brings the potential applicant back to your company's needs and how they can solve your problem.

Responsibilities

Succinctly define this person's respon-sibilities. What projects, tasks, or programs will they "own" as part of their day-to-day job? This section will also define what other teams or individuals the new hire will work with. Is this role collaborative, supporting, or a lead?

What are the action words for the position? Here are some words to consider:

Build	Establish
Report	Create
Manage	Train
Support	Design
Grow	Administer
Schedule	Monitor
Maintain	Research
Increase	Implement
Promote	Develop

Preferred Skill Set

This section of the Job Description identifies what you would like to see in a candidate, although these are not make-or-break skills. These are the negotiables. A candidate with all or most of these is more likely to be hired. But you may still consider a candidate without them, based on their other skills and experience.

Consider tools and systems here. Ideally, a new hire already knows how to use the same tools or software that your company utilizes. This will save you time and resources; but with the right candidate, you may be willing to provide paid training.

Requirements

These are the non-negotiables for the position. This section includes what the candidate must show up with on the first day: knowledge, experience, abilities, and strengths. These include working knowledge or proficiency with certain tools or software that you do not expect to provide training for, as well as any certification or licenses relevant to the position. Include not only what they should have experienced in previous positions but also personality traits that best align with the position.

Requirement Examples:

- outgoing and energetic
- professional written and verbal communication
- five years of experience with Google Docs
- QuickBooks® certification

Remember, be realistic with your requirements and be sure they correlate to the pay rate for the position. Expecting fifteen-plus years of experience in your industry or with a particular software is unrealistic if you are only offering entry-level pay.

Working Environment

This is the opportunity to share very specific details about the position. Provide more information about the location of work and expectations.

- Office or on-site: cubicle, corner office, warehouse, storefront, etc.
- Virtual: Will they be expected to participate in video calls? If so, be sure to require a quiet workspace with appropriate lighting/background.
- Hybrid: Provide the expectations of in-office and remote time (e.g., weekly in-person meetings, specific days in the office for hands-on work).

Think ahead to additional basic questions that a candidate would ask. Answering those here will save time and energy later in the process.

- What are the hour expectations (e.g., days, nights, weekends, or flexible)?
- What tools will the company provide (e.g., tablet or phone)?
- Are there any physical requirements? Does the position require someone to be on their feet all day or lifting a certain amount of weight on a regular basis?
- Are there uniform or dress code requirements? Explaining the daily dress code now may deter improperly dressed interviewees.
- What are the travel requirements (e.g., quarterly meetings, annual planning retreats, special events, or conferences)?

Pay and Benefits

We urge you to become comfortable talking about money. Be fully transparent with potential candidates about this position's pay and benefits. Expectations go both ways on a Job Description. You have expectations of the work the potential new hire will perform. On the other side, the candidate has expectations of how they will be compensated for that work. Transparency is needed on both sides.

Be up front with this information in the Job Description, and do not wait until the

Expectations go both ways on a Job Description.

interview-stage to discuss compensation. If this is something you need to keep confidential until later, the screening process discussed in detail in Chapter 4 is that opportunity. Don't waste your time, or a candidate's time, by not providing this essential figure prior to the interview.

While you mentioned key elements of the role in the beginning of the Job Description, reiterate if the position is full time, part time, or contracted and whether salaried or hourly. For a salaried position, share a "starting at" rate or salary range for annual compensation. Similarly, share a "starting at" or range for hourly compensation. If overtime is applicable, be sure to say so (e.g., "Frequent overtime available" or "Overtime during the busy season of …"). Also, state the pay rate for overtime (typically 1.5 times the hourly rate).

If there are other forms of compensation, describe those as well. The most common of these would be a commission structure or the potential for regular bonuses. Include the criteria for these, whether based on sales, performance, or some other metric.

Be specific about what benefits you offer, instead of a blanket statement such as "… and benefits."

- Health insurance
- Life/disability (or other) insurance
- 401(k) (with or without employer matching)

- Paid time off
- Paid holidays
- Tuition assistance
- Wellness programs
- Stock options
- Profit-sharing

If your company offers other perks worth listing, you can add them here. Some of these may include:

- Employee discounts
- Casual Fridays
- Catered lunches once a week
- On-site gym
- On-site childcare
- Allowance for personal development
- Shared reading library

How to Apply

Conclude your Job Description with how to apply. If you have an online automated system, provide that information. If résumés must be emailed, ask applicants to include a specific subject line to assist with inbox organization (this also tests the applicant's attention to detail).

If you are just beginning to automate your hiring process, we recommend establishing an email address solely devoted to hiring, such as hiring@ or jobs@[insert company domain]. This allows more than one person to manage the inbox, if needed, and streamlines the process. It also keeps other inboxes organized and free of clutter.

Ask for a cover letter, if desired. Typically, any critical items addressed in a cover letter will also be included in the résumé. We view the cover letter more as an opportunity for the candidate to sell themselves a bit more and add a personal touch. This is also where a candidate could provide clarity if there is a gap in their work history or something that needs more explanation. If the position requires excellent written communication, this is the first opportunity to assess the candidate.

Your instructions can be brief, like so:

> *To be considered for this position, email your résumé and cover letter to jobs@[insert company domain]. Please include the subject line "Strategic Assistant Application."*

Don't ask for references at this point. We will address references later in the process.

Legal and Compliance

At the end of the Job Description, add an Equal Employment Opportunity (EEO) statement. Some companies take this opportunity to also reiterate parts of their company culture. For example, Google's EEO statement per their website reads:

At Google, we don't just accept difference—we celebrate it, we support it, and we thrive on it for the benefit of our employees, our products and our community. Google is an equal opportunity employer. Employment at Google is based solely on a person's merit and qualifications directly related to professional competence. Google does not discriminate against any employee or applicant because of race, creed, color, religion, gender, sexual orientation, gender identity/expression, national origin, disability, age, genetic information, veteran status, marital status, pregnancy or related condition (including breastfeeding), or any other basis protected by law.

It is Google's policy to comply with all applicable national, state, and local laws pertaining to nondiscrimination and equal opportunity. The Company's EEO policy, as well as its affirmative action obligations, includes the full and complete support of the Company, including its Chief Executive Officer. Because it's just the right thing to do. We hope you think so, too.

Other companies utilize brevity with the simple statement:

[Insert company name] is an Equal Opportunity Employer.

The U.S. Equal Employment Opportunity Commission shares more information and resources on this topic online at eeoc.gov.

Also include any other verbiage that is necessary and appropriate for your company and the position. This could include information about background checks or drug screenings relevant to the job. Refer to federal and state laws to understand what is and isn't allowed by law, regarding candidate and employee privacy.

Background Check/Drug Screening Phrasing Samples:

All offers of employment are contingent upon the results of a job-related background check.

Candidates who have received an offer of employment will be required to undergo testing for commonly abused controlled substances in accordance with our company policy.

Tips:

Try to keep the Job Description to under three pages. Too many details and words may cause applicants to not fully absorb all the information. Remember from our introduction, communication actually begins before you ever hire. Do you want to communicate simplicity or complexity? Keeping the Job Description tight and to the point will increase the volume of applicants. Just be sure to balance the simplicity with pertinent details to immediately eliminate those who are not a good fit.

Keeping the Job Description tight and to the point will increase the volume of applicants.

Create a short summary for the position that you will use when posting the job. This needs to be a bit more eye-catching and entire the applicant to read further. The summary can be used for advertisement and sharing brief information about the opening, to then be followed up by the full Job Description.

Sample Job Description Summary:

> *Are you a strategic thinker who thrives on processes and organization? Are you searching for a work environment that values joy, growth, and lifelong learning? As a Strategic Assistant at Joy of Pursuit, your contributions will increase efficiency and accuracy in daily business operations. We need your skills of communication, time management, and emotional intelligence in order to continue to serve our clients beyond their expectations.*

> *Click below for full job description and information on how to apply.*

Following is a full example of an actual Job Description for the position of Strategic Assistant. If you are interested in a custom Job Description, reach out to us: Simplify@TheJoyOfPursuit.com.

Job Description Example:

Strategic Assistant

We are seeking a Strategic Assistant to work directly with our CEO and CFO performing a number of administrative duties. This is a full-time remote/work-from-home position with minimal travel. Starting salary of [$$$] with benefit options. The Strategic Assistant will interact directly with top-level clients, strategic partners, and team members, providing information and service to this wide range of internal and external contacts. Joy of Pursuit only seeks to hire individuals who possess our core values, which include:

1. Pursuing joy daily
2. Possessing an abundance mindset
3. Promoting grace-given gifts to serve others
4. Practicing lifelong learning
5. Preparing for success through accountability

The ideal candidate is highly self-motivated, professional, and capable of managing and prioritizing tasks in a fast-paced environment. Exceptional communication, calendar management, organizational skills, and follow-through are necessary for success in this role. The goal of this position is to keep projects moving, think clearly through processes and initiate next steps, remove or resolve barriers, streamline processes, and contribute to the overall efficiency and accuracy of the business.

JOB RESPONSIBILITIES:

- Manage individual calendars for CEO and CFO
- Maintain accuracy and be the point of contact for company-wide team and event calendars
- Schedule meetings, draft agendas, assist with meeting preparation, and anticipate needs for all calendar events
- Coordinate travel arrangements and plan itineraries
- Prepare internal and external documents for team and clients
- Manage electronic document filing system

PREFERRED SKILL SET:

- Work experience as a Strategic Assistant or similar role
- Understanding of how to work and communicate with different personality types
- Tech savvy with a willingness to learn and teach new programs
- Advanced knowledge of writing, marketing, and social media
- Experience with remote work and collaborating with virtual teams
- Working knowledge of Basecamp or a project management software

JOB REQUIREMENTS:
- Excellent and professional written and verbal communication skills
- Attention to detail and accuracy
- Resourceful/problem solver
- Exceptional efficiency and time management skills
- Strong working knowledge of Google Docs, Google Sheets, Google Calendar, and Zoom conferencing
- Personal character in accordance with the company's core values and beliefs
- Friendly and professional demeanor
- Professional/business-casual dress during meetings with clients and other external contacts
- Regular attendance at virtual meetings multiple times a week
- Upholds a strict level of confidentiality and discretion

WORKING ENVIRONMENT:
- Remote/work-from-home
- Quiet workspace with appropriate lighting and background for video calls
- US Eastern business hours—flexible working hours with an overlap to US EST business hours
- Timely response to emails, messages, and calls applicable to given situations
- Reliable high-speed Internet connection, phone, and PC or laptop running Windows 10/8 or Mac OS less than 3 years old with webcam capabilities
- Travel 1–3 times a year (with plenty of advance notice)

SALARY AND BENEFITS:
- Full time, salaried position
- Starting pay of [$$$]/annual, paid monthly
- Benefits:
  - Health insurance
  - 401(k) with matching
  - Two weeks paid vacation

To be considered for this position, email your résumé and cover letter to email@address.com, with the subject line "Strategic Assistant Application."

Chapter Three

Recruitment Strategy

If you think it's expensive to hire a professional, wait until you hire an amateur.

—Red Adair

Begin your candidate sourcing by leveraging the resources you already have. It is both practical and respectful to share a new job opening with those who currently work for you. Here are three reasons to share the job opening internally first:

1. Transparent communication about current business needs and growth is best.

2. Current team members may be interested in the position.

3. Employees make the best recruiters and references.

Internal Communication Example:

> *Dear Team,*
>
> *We are growing! Our hiring team is actively seeking a Strategic Assistant for our [insert person or department, e.g., CEO, sales department]. We greatly value your input and know you are the best at describing why we're great people to work with. Please share with anyone in your network who you think would be a good fit or could help spread the word about this open position. The job description is attached as a PDF, or information can be found here: [share link to*

online job posting or social media post].

After you have posted the job internally, communicate with your outside network. This will boost your recruitment efforts without added costs. Those who know you and your company are optimal references to explain why someone should want to work with you and apply for the job. Send the description to your friends and business acquaintances, requesting they share with others and send referrals your way.

Personal Communication Example:

Hi, friend!
My company is growing, and we are actively seeking a Strategic Assistant. I greatly value your input and know you have excellent business connections. Please share

with anyone in your network who you think would be a good fit or could help spread the word about this open position. I have attached the job description as a PDF, or information can be found here: [share link to online job posting].

Where to Post

If you don't already have a page on your company website with job information, now is the time to add it. Job seekers frequently look for this on sites of businesses they would like to work for. Also, someone may hear about a job opening with your company from a friend or colleague but not have seen the Job Description. This will likely be the first place they search for it.

Utilize all your business's social media accounts. Many social media platforms allow free job postings for businesses. If appropriate, share these posts to your personal social media to expand your reach.

By posting on social media, your team can easily share with their networks, increasing the **Share with the audience that already loves your brand.** views of the post. You'll also be sharing with an audience that already loves your company, understands what you do, and likely shares your values.

Once you have covered all internal, personal, and company-owned ways of sharing the job information, it is time to look externally for posting opportunities. Local business networking groups and job boards are a great next step. If you are not already a member of these groups, now is the perfect time to see what resources are locally available to you. Your local chamber of commerce is typically a good starting point for local recruitment efforts. If you have several openings and need to keep your candidate pipeline full, consider joining a local in-person job fair. This is outstanding exposure for your company and brand.

After you have utilized local connections for the job posting, move to online options for sharing information about the open position. Online networking groups relevant to your industry, whether with a free or paid membership, have many benefits. Establishing these associations now will give you another platform to share openings when you are ready to fill positions on your team.

The other online option for sharing information about your recruitment is large-scale job board sites. The possibilities are endless with these sites. However, we advise that you focus your sourcing efforts instead of posting to every site possible. It is worth a bit of research to see what online job boards are best for the type of position you are advertising.

Go to where your ideal candidate searches for jobs in your specific field. There are numerous niche job search sites. For example, one site may be the go-to option for technology experts, while another may be the best place to find a copywriter. Keep in mind that some online job boards require payment. Don't be discouraged if paid advertising is not in your budget; many online job sites have free postings available, at least for a trial period.

Chapter Four

Applicant Tracking and Screening

*People are not your most important asset.
The right people are.*

—Jim Collins

Now that you have defined and posted your open position, it's time to set up a system for tracking candidates as they work through the applicant funnel. Applicant Tracking Software (ATS) can be purchased, but these are not necessary for small businesses with a low hiring volume. We recommend the simplest option—a spreadsheet we call the Applicant Tracking Sheet—as seen here:

Applicant Tracking Sheet

Candidate	Date Applied	Sent Screening Questions	Completed Screening Questions	Passed Screening Questions	Sent Skills Assessment	Completed Skills Assessment	Passed Skills Assessment
John Smith	11/1/21	11/1/21	11/2/21	Yes	11/2/21	11/3/21	Yes
Suzy Green	11/1/21	11/1/21	11/2/21	Yes	11/3/21		
Amy Jones	11/2/21	11/2/21	11/2/21	Yes	11/3/21	11/5/21	No
Brad Robbins	11/4/21	11/4/21	11/5/21	Yes	11/5/21	11/6/21	Yes
Meg Stevens	11/4/21	11/4/21	11/6/21	No			
Rob White	11/8/21	11/9/21	11/10/21	No			
Andy Williams	11/9/21	11/9/21					
Carrie Miller	11/9/21	11/10/21	11/11/21	Yes	11/12/21	11/15/21	Yes
Grace Davis	11/11/21	11/11/21	11/12/21	No			
Matt Johnson	11/12/21	11/15/21	11/15/21	No			
Scott Lewis	11/15/21	11/15/21	11/17/21	Yes	11/18/21	11/19/21	No
Jackson Lee	11/15/21	11/16/21					
Angie Allen	11/16/21	11/17/21	11/17/21	Yes	11/18/21	11/18/21	Yes

Think of the Applicant Tracking Sheet as the hub where you'll easily be able to see how many applications have come in and where each candidate stands in the process. This will ideally link to files for each candidate with all information they submit.

You will also need a place to house résumés, cover letters, and assessments for easy retrieval as you evaluate candidates. We encourage you to collaborate with the appropriate members of your team during this process. To do so, set up shared folders and files so all information is in one central location in your digital storage or project management system. Establishing your applicant tracking method in an organized manner will ensure efficiency throughout this process.

Tip: Implement a file-naming system. Consistency will allow for better searchability of electronic files.

File-Naming System Sample:

Folder name:

- John Smith (the candidate's name)

File names:

- Résumé John Smith
- Cover Letter John Smith
- Skill Assessment John Smith

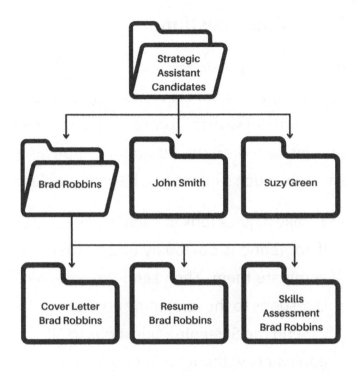

If your team is large enough to assist, candidate tracking is a duty you can delegate. Allow this team member to handle the initial steps of the hiring process. You can see progress updates by reviewing the Applicant Tracking Sheet.

Screening Questions

Now that you have résumés coming in, it's time to spend hours reviewing all of them, right? *No!* Not with this process. You have two options based on the number of applicants and how much support you have available:

1. Take a quick look at each résumé. If someone is obviously under-qualified, eliminate them. Then send the Screening Questions to the remaining applicants.
2. Send the Screening Questions to all applicants without taking the time to look at their résumés.

Screening Questions are an efficient way to collect data about the applicants that may not be listed on their résumés. Also, Screening Questions provide them the opportunity to expand on their skills and experience. This step (and the following Skills Assessment) are predictors of job performance. This is also when to share salary information if you didn't include it in the Job Description.

This technique also serves as a "self-screening" for the applicant in two ways:

1. Self-realization of under qualification may occur after the applicant reads the questions. As a result, they remove themselves from the selection process.
2. Failure to complete results in elimination. If the applicant is not willing to take five minutes to answer the questions, are they someone you would want to hire? Absolutely not.

Screening Questions can be completed in different ways, from pen and paper to online surveys. Google Forms is easy, accessible, and will compile the data into a spreadsheet for you.

You can use a variety of question types:

- Yes or no
- Rating scale
- Multiple choice
- Open-ended

Keep the questions brief and easy to understand and the number of open-ended questions to a minimum. The applicants should be able to complete the Screening Questions in under five minutes.

Criteria and Metrics

What questions to ask? Refer to the Job Description when defining what criteria you want to measure and what data to collect from the Screening Questions. As you craft the questions, think through what responses will or will not move someone to the next step.

Suggested Screening Questions:

- Years of experience (can apply to an industry, role, or tool)
- Knowledge level of tools/software (use a rating scale)
- Availability to begin position, if hired (e.g., "How soon can you start?")
- Experience managing a team size of 1–5, 5–10, 10+
- Describe an ideal workday

We advise you to include some non-negotiables from the Job Description. Even though they should be clearly listed, this is the perfect time to confirm that the applicant understands and pays attention to details. This confirmation will avoid the wasted time of reaching the interview stage with an applicant who doesn't meet the non-negotiable criteria.

Non-negotiables Examples:

- Willing to travel for work
- Available to work weekends, evenings, or take calls
- Starting hourly rate
- Required tools (e.g., webcam if working remotely)

To conclude the Screening Questions:

1. Request professional references. While some may have already provided these on their résumés, collecting the information here will allow you and your team to easily retrieve the references when needed.
2. Allow the applicant to add any additional information they want to share that isn't on their résumé or addressed in the previous questions.

When inviting applicants to complete your Screening Questions, continue to practice good communication. Inform them about how long the questions should take to complete and thank them for their interest in the position. Include your company's Core Values and/or Vision Purpose Statement as well (this will come into play if they make it to the interview stage).

Below is a sample email. Your team can simply copy and paste the same message for each candidate. Also, instruct your team to record on the Applicant Tracking Sheet the date the questions are sent and when answers are received.

Screening questions are the perfect time to confirm that the applicant pays attention to details.

Screening Questions Email Example:

> *Thank you for your interest in our Strategic Assistant position. We have received your résumé via [insert applicable info here]. The next step is for you to complete*

the attached Screening Questions. These questions should take less than five minutes to complete, and your answers will give us the opportunity to learn more about you. I have also attached our Core Values/Vision Purpose Statement to give you some insight into our company's purpose and culture.

Thank you for your time.
[Signature(s)]

Grading the Responses

Once you collect data that are easy to analyze, you (or your team) can review and grade the responses. This may be a task to delegate to someone on your team who can, at minimum, begin the process for you.

Start with the non-negotiables mentioned above. This will quickly eliminate individuals from the system and move them to the *no* pile. There is no need to read the responses to other questions if the required criteria are not met. You can indicate these non-negotiables by emboldening or changing their color on the spreadsheet (if applicable), making it easy to identify where to start.

This is especially important if you pay the person assisting **Start with the Non-negotiables.** you by the hour; you don't want them wasting their time on unqualified candidates.

After the unqualified applicants are removed, evaluate all responses for the remaining candidates. Again, if working in a spreadsheet, you can use colors to create an easy visual for comparison. For example, red for not qualified, yellow for proceeding cautiously, and green for good to go to the next step.

We recommend that after the first review, you select another team member to look over the information. This collaboration can identify any other applicants that need to go to the *no* list.

For those remaining, even if they seem to be a *maybe*, move them on to the next step.

Red Flags:

- All 10s on skill level for tools/software
- Refusal to add references
- Unprofessional references: mom, cousin, roommate, etc.

Tips:

- Attach the survey results (Google Sheet) to the Applicant Tracking Sheet for all candidates. This will keep all your hiring information in one file.
- On the Applicant Tracking Sheet, strike through any candidates you are not moving forward with.

• Pick up on cues not only from the candidate's answers but from HOW they answer. This may reveal a lack of attention to detail.

Question: Yes or No—Do you have experience with event planning? If yes, what size of event?

Answer: Yes.

Problem: The respondent didn't give the additional information requested.

• Send Core Values, Vision Purpose Statement, or additional information about the company along with the Screening Questions. Then reference this information in one of the questions. By doing so, you should cue the applicant to the importance of this information. (You'll learn more about how to use this as a prompt during a face-to-face interview later in Chapter 5.)

Strategic Assistant
Screening Questions

**After reviewing the Joy of Pursuit Core
Values, do you feel your values are in
alignment with ours?**   Yes   No

**Do you have experience working as a
part of a virtual team?**   Yes   No

**Do you have experience managing
multiple calendars?**   Yes   No

If yes, please elaborate:_____
_____
_____

**How many years of strategic assistant (or similar role)
experience do you have?**

None   <2 years   2-5 years   6-10 years   >10 years

If hired, when could you being work?
Immediately   Within 2 weeks   2-4 weeks   > 4 weeks

**Please rate your proficiency with these programs on a
scale of 1-10.**   1 = Never Used   10 = Very Proficient

Google Docs	1	2	3	4	5	6	7	8	9	10
Google Sheets	1	2	3	4	5	6	7	8	9	10
Google Calendar	1	2	3	4	5	6	7	8	9	10
Basecamp	1	2	3	4	5	6	7	8	9	10
Slack	1	2	3	4	5	6	7	8	9	10

**Please list 3 professional references, their contact
information, and relationship to you:**

1 _____
2 _____
3 _____

Skills Assessments

Now that you've sifted the résumés and answers to the Screening Questions, you have fewer applicants, and it's time to ask for a bit more effort from them. It can be relatively easy for candidates to write down their skills and proficiencies on paper. But *demonstrating* the skills reinforces their words with actions. This is where a Skills Assessment comes into play.

The goal of this tool is to allow the applicant to prove their skills that relate to the job and to remove assumptions about their knowledge.

Demonstrating the skills reinforces their words with actions.

This step should come prior to dedicating your valuable time to interviews.

A Skills Assessment doesn't need to knock your socks off. It is simply an opportunity for the applicant to show they are competent in some of the basics and, therefore, worthy of your time to interview.

When crafting your Skills Assessment, consider these two components:

1. *what* to assess
2. *how* to assess

When choosing *what* skills to assess, refer back to the action words used in the Responsibilities portion of the Job Description: *develop, create, monitor, report,* etc. Also, revisit and note the Requirements of the position from the job description.

The type of Skills Assessment you use can vary greatly depending on the role. Here are some ideas to get you started:

- use of basic software or tool (e.g., Microsoft Office, Google Workspace, social media platforms)

- writing and/or editing skills
- portfolios or examples of work for creative positions (e.g., graphic design, web design, photography, videography)
- general knowledge of the role (e.g., fundamentals of a marketing plan, information to ask attendees for an event, metrics members of a sales team should monitor, components of project management)

Once you have the basis of what you will assess, think through the details of *how* to assess. This may be used as an opportunity to determine the candidate's attention to detail and proficiency with the functions of a specific tool. This also removes any assumptions, such as *everyone knows how to use Google Sheets* or other widely known programs.

Technology and free online tools make the options for how you assess the candidates' skills limitless. Here are some assessment options and examples of how you might use them:

Video or Voice Recordings

Video and audio recordings are perfect assessments for jobs requiring exceptional verbal communication. For example, if you are hiring a salesperson for a particular product line, provide the applicant with the basic information and ask them to record a one- to three-minute sales pitch.

Shared Online or Attached Documents

Let's say the open position is for the lead of the marketing department where all team members work a hybrid in-office/remote schedule. Request that the applicant create a sample agenda for the team's weekly meeting, including key metrics to be reported.

To take this assessment a step further, think through the necessity of online communication due to the hybrid work environment. Ask for the sample agenda to be created as a Google Doc, including specifics such as document title, sharing capabilities, and link. This will give you additional criteria to measure their attention to detail.

Screenshots and Screencasts

When the role requires social media management, request a screencast of the applicant demonstrating where to find specific items on your company's social media page, such as upcoming events or the link to the job position they are applying for. Other assessments could be more in-depth, asking the applicant to create a private social media group on a specific platform and adjust particular settings. Overall, this will allow the applicant to demonstrate their proficiency with the social media platform.

When it comes time to review the completed Skills Assessments, one way to save time is to request screenshots of specific items in the assessment. This allows you or your team to quickly scan the screenshots to see if they match the expected results of the assessment.

If they do, then you can delve more into the assessment, such as watching the entire screencast or reviewing documents in detail. If the screenshots do not coincide with expectations, then you know that candidate will not move forward, and you save a great deal of time.

Save time by requesting screenshots.

If you are hiring for a position that requires someone tech savvy with good research skills, don't overexplain the assessment. This is the opportunity to see how much effort the candidate is willing to put forth. For example, we once asked job candidates to create a screencast while demonstrating certain functionalities of a social media platform. This remote position required someone who was tech savvy, a problem solver, and capable of working independently without a lot of handholding. We purposely did not provide a definition or explanation of a screencast. We had several applicants make it to this step in the process. Here are responses from two:

Candidate 1 responded with several questions, including, *"I don't know what a screencast is. How do I do that?"*

Candidate 2 provided the screencast, as requested, with all items well demonstrated. Later during an interview, this candidate shared that he initially was not familiar with screencasts, but he researched it and called a friend to ask advice for best practices. After educating himself on the basics of this tool, he completed the assessment.

The first candidate didn't move past the Skills Assessment stage. She quickly showed us she was not tech savvy. But more importantly, we learned that when this candidate faced a hurdle, her response was to run back with questions before taking a moment to figure it out for herself.

When the job requires the ability to work independently and remotely, it's vital that small hang-ups be resolved on their own. A quick Internet search—"what is a screencast"—would have answered her question. It also would have been much quicker than emailing us and awaiting a response.

It's vital that small hangups be resolved on their own.

On the other hand, the second candidate was top of the list to be hired, and he turned into a star employee.

A Skills Assessment should take a bit more time than the Screening Questions, but try to keep it to under fifteen minutes, depending on the position. Communicate the time expected to complete the assessment in the request email. Keep the tone of communication positive and even a bit celebratory.

Convey that the candidate is doing well in your process and moving to the next

Providing clarity will keep them motivated.

level. This encouragement will assist with relationship building prior to meeting and keep candidates interested in your position.

Also, let candidates know that this is the final step before interviewing. This will assure them that the entire process isn't endless emails back and forth and that a face-to-face meeting is forthcoming if they do well with this assessment. Providing this clarity will keep them motivated and support a positive candidate experience.

Skills Assessment Email Example:

> *Thank you for completing our initial screening questions for the Strategic Assistant position, and congratulations on moving into the next phase of our hiring process! This phase gives you an opportunity to demonstrate your knowledge of some of the programs and basic tasks necessary for this position. We know your time is valuable and appreciate you taking the time to complete the Skills Assessment (see below or attached). It should take less than 15 minutes to complete. Again, we appreciate your interest in this position and your effort given to our hiring process. This*

assessment is the last step in our process prior to moving into the interview stage for this position.

Just as it happens with some candidates during the previous Screening Questions, there will be some who opt out of the process at this stage. They may have exaggerated their skills on their résumé and Screening Questions. Now that they are being asked to demonstrate the skill, they know they can't. Or they may not want to put forth the effort, which means they would not be a good hire.

Strategic Assistant
Skills Assessment

Please record a screencast as you complete these tasks:

- Compose a new email
  - Subject line: Your Name Skills Assessment
  - The email will be to: hiringemail@
  - In the body of the email (using a numbered list) share 3 words that describe your style of work

- Create a Google Doc
  - Title it the same as your email subject
  - Create a sample meeting agenda including:
    - Bullet points
    - Variations of fonts and text color for headings
  - Demonstrate how to make a comment in the document
  - Demonstrate how to make suggestions for edits
  - Create a link to share the document allowing others to edit
  - Place the link in the email started above

- Create a Google Sheet
  - Create sample headings for 5 columns
  - Fill sample data into 10 rows
  - Hyperlink your Google Doc from above in one of the sample data cells
  - Color column C and row 5 yellow
  - Name first sheet Sample 1
  - Add 2 more sheet tabs and rename them Sample 2 & Sample 3
  - Copy & paste data from Sample 1 to other sheets
  - On Sample 2 change yellow cells to blue
  - Take a screenshot only of the filled cells on Sample 2
  - Place screenshot in the email started above

- Create a sample event on Google Calendar
  - Title the event "Rob Smith Proposal"
  - Set date to March 14th, 2022 @ 3 pm EST. Duration of 90 minutes
  - Take a screenshot of the details
  - Place screenshot in the email started above
  - Also in the email, write a short message to the client Rob Smith inviting him to the meeting above. Italicize the message to Rob and change the font color to set it apart from the rest of your email message.

Stop screencast. Then send the email with the complete screencast and other items above.

Evaluating the Skills Assessment

Evaluation will vary depending on the type of Skills Assessment. If the work can be viewed objectively (i.e., *yes/completed correctly* or *no/completed incorrectly*), this is a task to delegate to someone assisting you in the hiring process. Only the candidate who measures well on the metrics will be brought "up the ladder" for review.

For the example of Strategic Assistant, each item on the assessment will receive a *yes* or *no* to reflect whether the task was completed correctly or incorrectly. For these items, you can use a scale similar to this to determine if the candidate will progress to the interview stage or needs a closer evaluation:

- 90% correct = *yes*
- 75-89% = *maybe*
- Below 75% = *no*

For the *maybes*, look closer at what was missed. It could be a small oversight or a more significant issue. Pull all of the candidate's information and evaluate it in totality. Review the skills they claimed on their résumé. Compare the assessment to the applicant's Screening Questions responses.

Review the skills they claimed on their résumé. Do their initial responses of skill level match with what was demonstrated during the assessment? Reviewing their résumé and answers to Screening Questions along with the Skills Assessment will either highlight or diminish your concerns. Get a second opinion from a team member who is assisting in the hiring process if necessary.

For Skills Assessments that may be more subjective, define the basic criteria that would be minimum requirements for the role. In the above suggestion of a video recording for someone applying for a sales position, make sure the applicant reiterated all pertinent information in their recording, such as product name, price point, and how to purchase. Beyond that, evaluate for clear communication and pronunciation and a speed that is enthusiastic but easy to understand. Beyond those basic elements, you can look more subjectively at passion and creativity.

When reviewing a portfolio of design work for a creative position, don't overlook the details, including grammar, spelling, and punctuation (if applicable). If you asked for specific design samples based on an objective, be sure the work meets the requirements and all the details are intact.

You now have additional information about each candidate to help you select which are worth taking the time to interview. Résumés, Screening Questions, Skills Assessments, as well as promptness in completing steps in the process and friendliness of correspondence can add to the appeal of a candidate. Once you and your team have made your final decisions about who is a *yes*, it's time to move to the interview stage.

Chapter Five

The Interview

You can't teach employees to smile.
They have to smile before you hire them.

—Arte Nathan

The number of candidates who completed all steps in the hiring process is likely drastically fewer than those who initially sent in résumés. This is evidence of the process working. While you or your team have taken time to email them and review responses, that time is significantly less than attempting to sift through résumés, then schedule and conduct interviews with all the *maybes* on your list.

When inviting the candidate to an interview, be sure to include all the relevant information:

- Who from the team will be in the interview and their titles?
- How long the interview is expected to last?
- Where will the interview be conducted (in person, phone interview, or video call)?

Tip: If using video for the interview, communicate your expectations.

Interview Email Example:

Thank you for your continued interest in our Strategic Assistant position. We appreciate your commitment to our hiring process. After reviewing your résumé,

Screening Questions, and Skills Assessment, we would like to elevate you to the interview phase.

For this initial interview, you will meet with [name, title, position] and [name, title, position]. The interview will be a video call lasting not more than 45 minutes. Please know that our team greatly values face-to-face interaction. Be prepared to join this interview with your camera on from a quiet, well-lit area.

Listed below are date and time options. Please let us know which slot you prefer. Call details will be sent once time is confirmed.

We look forward to meeting you! [Signature(s)]

Who Participates in the Interviews?

This depends on the size of your team. Ideally, you will have input from a minimum of three team members. These individuals should be involved in the hiring process, though given the size of your team, one person may wear two or more hats.

1. Human resource representative/Hiring Manager
2. Member from the executive/leadership team
3. Manager or lead, to whom the candidate will report

The potential fourth team member to collaborate with during the interview process would be someone who is familiar with the role and will work directly with the new hire.

We recommend a two-round interview process with two of the above-mentioned team members in each interview. If you only have three people available, have the team member who is leading the hiring process sit in both interviews.

Round one should always include the manager or lead the candidate will be directly accountable to. To protect your Executive Team's time, save their participation for round two, if the first interview goes well.

Depending on your team dynamics, the HR representative can sit in both meetings or one. The collaborative team member would sit in the other meeting.

If possible, don't conduct one-on-one interviews. Here are three reasons why:

1. Collaborative hiring—Two people will pick up on different responses, mannerisms, highlights, or concerns during the interview. This will allow for good discussion and sharing of information post-interview.

2. Better candidate experience—The potential time and anxiety of sitting through three or four interviews with different team members does not make this a streamlined process for the candidate. For someone who values their time—and may be working at another job and making special arrangements to be available—two meetings will always be better than three or four.

3. Shortens the process—Scheduling two interviews will reduce the overall timeline. Transition time between interviews and scheduling additional meetings add days or even weeks to the hiring process.

What if you are a team of one? Lean on your inner circle, those you trust the most and who know the most about your business. Or reach out to us for consultation and interview assistance.

Interview Prep

Compliance, ScoreCARD, and Agendas

Prior to the interview, review the candidate's information (résumé, Screening Questions, Skills Assessment, and any other notable communication) to refresh your memory. This will help you identify items you would like to expand upon and define your ScoreCARD (more information to come in the next section). Provide all of these details to the round one interview team.

It's vital to know what questions *NOT* to ask during an interview. Some may be too personal or inappropriate, and others may indicate that you are attempting to discriminate. So, be sure you are up to date on what is and is not allowed. Everyone on your team who is involved in the interview process needs to be informed on legal stipulations

It's vital to know what questions NOT to ask during an interview.

and ethical guidelines prior to beginning interviews.

Below are examples of questions to avoid. Note that this is not a fully exhaustive list:

- Are you married?
- What is your maiden name?
- Have you changed your name?
- Do you go to church?
- How old are you?
- What year did you graduate?
- Do you have kids? What are their ages? Do you plan to have kids? Are you pregnant?
- What country are you from?
- How do you feel about working for a woman?
- What is your sexual orientation?
- Do you have any chronic medical conditions?

The two most vital laws to know related to employment discrimination are listed here:

> 1. *Title VII of the Civil Rights Act of 1964 prohibits employment discrimination based on race, color, religion, sex, and national origin.*
>
> 2. *The Americans with Disabilities Act of 1990 prohibits employment discrimination against a qualified individual with a disability.*

We recommend visiting the U.S. Equal Employment Opportunity Commission at eeoc.gov for additional details and to ensure you have a full understanding of these laws.

Interview Tool

Just as the Screening Questions and Skills Assessment provided consistency when evaluating the candidate, you will use a similar tool throughout the interview process. The Interview ScoreCARD will assist with an objective assessment of the candidate by all team members who participate in the interviews.

Regardless of the position, all ScoreCARDs will have some of the same basic components. Begin with the Job Description when crafting the ScoreCARD, just as you did with the previous screening tools. When scoring in each category, consider the following questions:

ScoreCARD Categories

Culture

1. Does the candidate share your company values and fit with your culture?
2. Would bringing this person on your team disrupt your culture in a negative way?

Ability

1. Do they have the time, emotional, intellectual, and educational capacities for this role?
2. Are they available mentally and physically to fill this role?

Role

1. Can they articulate a clear understanding   of   the   role   and expectations?
2. Was there anything they said during the interview that made you believe they don't meet the specific requirements for this role?

Desire

1. Do they truly want to work in this role?
(Make sure they aren't just looking to get
their foot in the door.)
2. Are they excited for this particular role or
just looking for a paycheck?

To continue with the goals of objectivity and
efficiency, we recommend using a numeric
score of 1–10 for each of the above items on
the ScoreCARD. If the score is below a 7, ask
for a brief explanation of the ranking from the
hiring team member.

For somewhat more open-ended and
subjective input, ask the interviewer to
give two to three words or phrases that
immediately come to mind to describe the
candidate.

The last item for the interviewer to complete
on the ScoreCARD is a simple question:

"Would you hire?" This is the ultimate summation of all the above information.

Leave space for any notes the interviewer may want to jot down at the bottom of the ScoreCARD.

Here is an example of a completed ScoreCARD.

Interview ScoreCARD

Culture
- Does the candidate share your company values and fit with your culture?
- Would bringing this person on your team disrupt your culture in a negative way?

Ability
- Do they have the emotional, time, intellectual, and educational capacities for this role?
- Are they available mentally and physically to fill this role?

Role
- Can they articulate a clear understanding of the role and expectations?
- Was there anything they said during the interview that made you believe they don't meet the specific requirements for this role?

Desire
- Do they truly want it to work in this role? (Make sure they aren't just looking to get their foot in the door.)
- Are they excited for this particular role or just looking for another paycheck?

Candidate _Brad Robbins_   **Position** _Strategic Assistant_
Interviewer _Carol Burns_   **Date** _11/8/21_

Rate on each component. 10 being an ideal fit.

Culture	1	2	3	4	5	6	7	8	(9)	10
Ability	1	2	3	4	5	6	7	(8)	9	10
Role	1	2	3	4	5	6	7	8	(9)	10
Desire	1	2	3	4	5	6	7	8	9	(10)

2-3 Words or phrases top of mind to describe the candidate
Prepared
Energetic
REALLY wants the job

Would hire? (Yes)   No   Maybe

Other notes or concerns
Overall great interview. Can be talkative - keep him on track during the 2nd interview.

Tips:

Use a Google Form for each interviewer to complete. Add the results to another tab on your Applicant Tracking Sheet from Chapter 4 to keep all information together for effortless retrieval.

When scheduling the interviews, block time on the interviewers' calendars to complete the ScoreCARD, debrief, and immediately submit their reports to the hiring team after the interview. Delaying the completion of the ScoreCARD may allow parts of the interview to be forgotten. Furthermore, submitting the ScoreCARD findings late to the hiring team will slow down the entire interview timeline.

Remember, interviews are a two-way street. The candidate is also interviewing you and your company to decide if they want the job. Show up prepared, remain engaged, and show the candidate that you value their time.

Choose one team member to lead the interview. This person will start and end the interview and is responsible for keeping the conversation on track. Make a list of specific questions you want to ask during the interview.

Be sure to ask a variety of questions so that you cover all the main topics from the ScoreCARD: skills, work experience, personality, value fit, coachability, emotional capacity, etc. Once you have identified specific questions to ask, be sure to do so for all candidates. This consistency will provide better data for fair applicant evaluations.

Keep in mind that a charismatic personality can easily sway opinions.

Keep in mind that a charismatic personality can easily sway opinions. You must dig deep with your questions and look past how well someone sells themselves.

Interview: Round One

If possible (and appropriate for the position), conduct the first interview via online video chat (Zoom, Skype). This saves and respects everyone's time. Utilize a ScoreCARD and add any notes or questions to the bottom.

Agenda for the Interview

Introduction

Introduce all team members attending the meeting. Let each person share who they are and why they are there. Will they work directly with the candidate? Are they overseeing the entire hiring process?

Get to Know the Candidate

Begin the interview with a very broad and open-ended question to get the conversation flowing.

Open-ended Question Example:

Tell us why you are interested in this position.

This conversation-starter allows nerves to settle and gives the candidate the opportunity to share whatever is top of their mind coming into the interview.

Structured Questions about Skills and Experience

Now move into more specific and targeted questions. These can be about work history or experience using certain tools. Reference the list you made when preparing for the interview.

Specific Question Example:

On your Screening Questions, you rated your knowledge of [insert tool/software] as a nine. Can you elaborate on your experience with this and in what capacity you have used it?

Company Culture Compatibility Questions

Remember earlier we mentioned using your company values in the interview process? This one question has revealed more to us in interviews than we ever expected. We've encountered candidates who have printed this information in preparation to talk about it and reference it clearly in interviews. Other candidates tried to fudge their way through, and some have been great at thinking on their feet.

Culture Question Example:

> *After reviewing our [Core Values, Mission Statement, or whatever information you sent them about the company], what resonates most with you?*

If you share this information when inviting the applicant to complete the Screening Questions and then reference it again in the actual questions, a perceptive person will recognize this as essential knowledge. Therefore, be prepared to discuss it during the interview.

Candidate Questions

Always allow the candidate to ask questions. Their questions can speak volumes to their personality, hopes, or concerns about the job. If a candidate has no questions for you, this may be a red flag, depending on the position and company culture.

Conclusion

Wrap up the interview by thanking the applicant for their time and interest. Do not leave a candidate hanging without knowing when you will be in touch again. Continue the clear communication we have highlighted repeatedly by letting them know the next steps.

Sample Conclusion Script:

Thank you for your time today. We appreciate the opportunity to learn more about you. We are continuing to interview other candidates and will be in touch with a decision by [insert deadline].

After the interview, take time to immediately debrief with the other team member(s) and complete your ScoreCARDs. Add items that may be possible concerns to specifically address during the next round of interviewing. Discuss positives and negatives. Most importantly, reflect on the original goal of the position. Will this person solve the problem you identified in the first step of this process? Decide—individually and together—if you think the candidate is a *yes, no,* or *maybe.*

If the consensus is *no,* be sure to let the candidate know within one business day. We share more on how to send this news to the applicant in the next chapter.

If the decision is *yes* or *maybe*, notify the appropriate team members and move the candidate to round two. Share with those conducting the second interview any items you want to address during the next interview. Bring any team members up to speed on the candidate if they didn't participate in the previous round's interview.

Is a second interview really necessary? This, of course, depends on the position, but it is highly recommended. Even if you already know you want to hire the candidate, still proceed with the second interview. Make sure they "show up" the way they did in the first round. You can always keep this one short, and if all goes well, offer them the job face-to-face.

Interview: Round Two

Follow the same agenda as round one, but you'll want to ask fresh questions in the second round. Have those questions prepared and available to those conducting the interview ahead of time. Be sure to address any specific follow-up items identified by the first interviewers. Don't forget to refresh the interviewer who wasn't in round one on what *not* to ask as well. Use the ScoreCARD and debrief with your colleagues immediately following the interview.

If necessary, you may need to meet with all interviewers from both rounds. Many situations may call for such a meeting, given the dynamics of the position and candidate(s). It may be that one interviewer is not convinced that the candidate is qualified. Or two or more candidates have made it through both rounds. Now the team must choose which candidate will be the best solution for the team. A group discussion can bring clarity here. Do not feel pressured to make the definitive decision yet. Move to the next step and reference-check your top two or three candidates. This step will likely elevate one candidate above their competition.

In other situations, everyone involved is one hundred percent confident you have the right person for the role, making the decision easy. Once you agree on this top candidate, you can move forward with checking their references.

Check References

Why check references?

It may be tempting to skip this step if you feel good about the applicant and are ready to hire them. But if you have made it this far in the process, it is worth the time to check references. While this step will likely validate what you have already learned about the candidate, keep in mind that it could make you aware of something you didn't know, saving you time, money, and headache down the road. Also, a reference check can help level the playing field for candidates who are introverted and not as skilled at "selling themselves" as other, more charismatic competing candidates may be.

As with all the previous steps, utilize a template to keep all reference checks consistent. You will see an example below of a completed reference check.

Begin the call by sharing information about yourself—your name, who you work for, and why you are calling. Let them know that you have a few questions that should only take five to ten minutes and how much you appreciate their time.

Next, verify and gather facts about the candidate, their relationship to the reference, and previous employment information. Then move to more subjective questions. You should take into consideration the possible bias of the reference (both good and bad). If you want answers beyond "sure, she's a team player," you'll have to ask very specific questions.

We recommend the method of asking for a numerical ranking of the candidate's skills and then follow up with asking for a short explanation. This will keep the reference focused on the specifics of what you're asking and also allow for possible red flags to surface. End the call by giving the reference a chance to share anything else they would like to add. Use the provided template to guide you through the reference check. You can make this digital using Google Forms to easily share information among your team.

Reference Check

Candidate Brad Robbins _____ **Date of Call** 11/17/21 _____

Reference Name Susan Alexander _____

What Is your relationship to the candidate? Both assisted managers In the same department

How long did you work with each other? 3 years

What duties did the candidate perform? Screening phone calls Managed calendar, prepared presentations, & other assistant duties

Can you verify details of start and end date, position/title?
unsure of start date (prior to her start). Executive Assistant

Rate the following traits/abilities 1-10 and give a brief explanation

9 Reliability Punctual and dependable

10 Organizational Skills Highly organized

9 Communication Never had any Issues

10 Accountability Always owns his mistakes.

8 Teamwork A team player, but likes to take the lead at times

6 Withstand stress Could get flustered when stressed

8 Adaptability Not a quick learner, but always willing

In what areas do you feel the candidate needs to improve?
Not overreacting to stress before knowing all the information.

Is there anything else should I know about the job candidate?
Loves talking to people. Usually a strength, but may need to be focused at times

Other notes or concerns:
Overall a happy co-worker who was good to work with

Social Media and Online Candidate Evaluation

Beyond calling the candidates' references, you can do your own research online. There are some important aspects to keep in mind when researching a candidate online. You will need structure and parameters in place to keep your research to facts and business and not introduce bias or questionable ethics.

Here are five basic rules to follow:

1. Remember the source. Online information may not always be accurate, up to date, or one hundred percent reliable.
2. Choose the team member to conduct this research who can be objective and set aside personal bias. They must have the capacity to make fair decisions.
3. Only conduct an online/social media evaluation after interviewing the candidate.

4. Lack of social media accounts should not affect your hiring decision unless it is required to fulfill the job duties.

5. Most importantly, remember the objective: is the candidate suitable for this job?

The objective is not to find out if you agree with their politics, what they do in their personal time, what their home looks like, their taste in music, or the name of their dog.

Keep it strictly about business and fact-checking. Search to confirm information about their previous employer: does the company exist, and does the candidate's previous position line up with the company's website or social media? Online sources can assist with verifying or denying claims the applicant has made.

Bottom line: do not look for or take into consideration any information on topics that you would not ask about in an interview.

Of course, conduct any type of necessary background check. This may be required for certain positions, such as a childcare worker, or relevant to the job and industry. Ask the candidate verbally for permission during the interview process if you plan to conduct a background check. Then follow up with a written background check authorization form. If the candidate's Social Security number or other government-issued identification is needed, follow all applicable state and local laws for transmitting and disposal of this information.

Making the Decision

It's decision time. To hire or not to hire?

You may have a clear front runner for this position, and if so, the decision is already made. But if you are evaluating two or more candidates, take time with your hiring team to fully review and discuss each of the candidates. After following the steps of this system, you have collected a great deal of information about the candidate. Utilizing ScoreCARDs will remove bias and promote data-driven decisions. Data will assist with equal evaluation of all skills necessary for the job and not allow for one or two personal qualities to dominate. Don't hire someone just because you like them; hire them because they are the right person for the role.

Chapter Six

Post-interview

*Hiring the wrong people is the fastest way
to undermine a sustainable business.*

—Kevin J. Donaldson

Extending the Offer

Now that you have found your ideal
candidate, it's time to extend the offer. If you
have a candidate who is a close second, don't
dismiss them yet. Wait until the top candidate
has accepted the offer. Typically, the offer
is extended via email, but you could also
call the candidate, if you feel it appropriate.

If you do verbally offer the position to the candidate, be sure to follow up with an email so everything is stated in writing. The written offer will include important details that you do not want misunderstood.

When extending the offer, remember that it is still only an *offer*. The candidate could decline. Maybe they **If you have a candidate who is a close second, don't dismiss them yet.** have thought it over and decided the job is not for them. It is also possible that they interviewed for several positions and were offered the job of their dreams just hours before.

When inviting someone to join your team, it is essential to reiterate a few specifics of the job. Be sure to include the job title, compensation, and benefits information in your offer. Also ask when they would be available to begin if they accept the position. If you discussed the timing during the interview, now is the time to confirm it. Know what your onboarding process is (what steps come next, as well as a timeline) if they agree to join your team. Clear communication is vital to set up your new employee for success.

Onboarding Checklist

New Hire Communications

☑ Create and share first-day schedule.

☑ Remind about documents that need to be provided (i.e., picture ID).

☑ Send link to any documents that can be completed electronically.

☐ Share information for who their point of contact person will be.

☑ Give link to team handbook (include organizational chart).

☐ Provide email and software access details to new hire.

☐ Invite new hire to all events, calendars, regularly scheduled meetings, etc., making sure important dates are notated with plenty of notice.

☐ Allow access to to-do lists, goals, or other planning documents to set new hire up for a great start.

☐ Share three most important objectives for the new hire for a set time frame (first week, month, quarter).

☐ Schedule evaluation follow up.

Team Communications

☑ Introduce and welcome the new hire to the whole team, including role title, department, etc.

☐ Set up email and software access (calendar, office communication software, etc.).

☑ Schedule meeting with HR department to confirm all paperwork is complete and explain compensation method and benefit options.

☐ Add to any team group chats, documents, and/or projects.

☐ Organize departmental meeting for face-to-face introductions.

☐ Arrange cross-departmental meetings for key roles that integrate with new hire.

Job Offer Email Example:

It was a pleasure to speak with you during your interview. We appreciate your time and effort during this process over the last couple of weeks. Our team feels that you would be a great fit for the Strategic Assistant position, and we would like to invite you to join us!

Starting pay is [$$$], with [insert benefits package information]. If you accept the position, we would like to begin your onboarding process on [date]. This date can be flexible, if needed, to accommodate your schedule.

Thank you again for your time. Please let me know if you have any questions.

Negotiations

After extending the offer, it is possible that the candidate makes a counteroffer and initiates a negotiation. Be prepared for this. If you have wiggle room with your compensation rate or benefits, establish your limits ahead of time. If you know there is zero capacity for negotiations, let the candidate know. Another strategy is to find middle ground with the candidate. Let them know that after the first thirty to ninety days, they will be evaluated. If they have proven they are the right fit for the position and provide the solution to your initial problem, they will receive a raise at that point in time. It is absolutely reasonable to expect a candidate to prove themselves during an initial set time frame.

But on the other side of that, be sure you follow through with your promises. State in writing how long the candidate will work until they are evaluated as well as a possible range of increase in compensation. Allow yourself enough time to fully evaluate them in their new position. You might assign them certain projects or define specific goals to meet, or you could leave it to the tasks defined on the Job Description. For a process to track evaluations and onboarding, check out the next book in *The Team Solution Series*, *The Onboarding Process* at TheJoyOfPursuit.com/Books.

Sometimes negotiations are best done in person or at least over the phone. Don't hesitate to schedule a quick follow-up call with the candidate if needed. If you do this, be sure to follow up with the newly agreed-upon terms in writing.

Negotiation Follow-up Email Example:

> *Thank you for your time today. For clarity, I want to follow up in writing with our agreement. For the position of Strategic Assistant, your starting pay and benefits package*

is [$$$]. We will evaluate your performance in this position sixty days from your start date. At that time, depending on the results of the evaluation, your compensation has the potential to increase to [$$$].

We look forward to onboarding with you next week.

Not Hired

After each step in the process, you will move some applicants to the *no* pile. Be sure to always close the loop with these candidates. While this may seem like a waste of time, it's important for your company's reputation, and it's just good manners. Again, communication is of utmost importance.

Provide constructive feedback, when appropriate. If a candidate doesn't meet the required skill set (or was just beat out by a better candidate), but they are in alignment with your culture and someone you would like to have on your team if they had more experience or training, let them know. This will encourage them to apply for future positions. Maybe they'll work to build the skills they lack and will fit in a similar role in a couple of years. Or they might be perfect for a different job you're hiring for in the future. Furthermore, good communication may allow you to approach the candidate for new positions in the future.

Reputation is important— protect yours with considerate communication.

Keeping records of all applicants will allow you to re-engage them for other or future positions.

When an applicant feels valued during the hiring process, even if not selected, they will be more likely to say good things about your company or at least not speak ill of it. It's a small world, and you never know when you will cross paths with this person again or be in need of their services. A simple email thanking them for their time and providing closure will go far. Reputation is important—protect yours with considerate communication. Lastly, remember that sometimes your new hire does not work out. Don't burn bridges with your second choice. You may be coming back to them in a few weeks or a few months to see if they are still interested in the position.

Rejection Email Example:

> *Thank you for contributing your time and attention to this application process. This email is to inform you that we will not continue with an interview at this time, but we are grateful for your interest in [company name]. We are looking for a candidate with more experience in [skill].*

If another position in our company opens that we feel you are a match for, we will be in touch in the future.

Be sure to make notes of who you would consider for future openings in your Applicant Tracking Sheet.

Chapter Seven

Wrap-up and Resources

Time spent on hiring is time well spent.

—Robert Half

Troubleshooting

If at any point during the process you determine a lack of interest or qualified candidates for the job, take a step back and look at previous steps to evaluate. It is okay to adjust and reconfigure. Be sure to not do this alone, though. Bring your hiring team together to discuss. It could also be beneficial to bring in a fresh set of eyes to look things over. Here are a few common items you may want to reassess:

- Job posting location—Remember to go where your ideal candidate looks for jobs. Take time to research this. Try a different online job board if you are not happy with the results from your first choice.
- Position title—Does it clearly communicate the role? Does it use verbiage that some would find diminishing or intimidating?
- Skills Assessment—Is it too lengthy or in-depth for the role?
- Realistic expectations—Is the required skill level appropriate for the offered compensation?

Remember to keep expectations relevant for the position. If hiring a c-suite employee, the applicants will expect a longer and more in-depth hiring process. When hiring a part-time employee for entry-level work, keep the expectations and process appropriate. A Skills Assessment for an entry-level position should be brief and at a basic level.

That's a Wrap!

Remember to keep the process moving. It is never wise to rush a hiring decision. Yet, it is also unwise to stall the hiring process. Before you advertise your job opening, have all the subsequent steps ready to be implemented. Staying organized will allow you and your team to have all candidate data accessible for easy retrieval. Know how you will evaluate the data collected. Have a firm understanding of what is and isn't negotiable for the position. Being confidently prepared with all steps will allow you to keep the hiring process moving once it's initiated, avoiding communication gaps, incomplete candidate tracking, and inconsistent metrics. This will result in better recruitment engagement, quicker hiring decisions, and saving time and resources. You will be less likely to lose a candidate to another job opening.

It's important to take time to wrap up your hiring search. Save all the information you have collected, résumés, and candidate tracking in one easy-to-access digital file for later. Remove the job posting on job boards, social media sites, and your company's website. Also, make a point to gather feedback from those involved. What worked well? Any areas for improvement? Make note of these for the next time you have a position to fill.

Now that you've worked through *The Hiring Process*, you have everything you need to make the best hiring decisions. You can duplicate the Job Description, Screening Questions, Skills Assessments, Applicant Tracking Sheet, and all the email correspondence and adjust accordingly for the specific position.

Continue with clear communication and setting expectations. Onboarding is a crucial step in employee retention. Put in the effort to develop a stellar onboarding process that will set your new hire up for success.

The Hiring Process Checklist

☑ Capacity check your team

☑ Choose who on your team will collaborate on the process

☑ Develop job description

☐ Write Screening Questions

☐ Create Skills Assessment

☐ Set up Applicant Tracking System

☐ Share the open position with your team

☐ Post/advertise job opening

☐ Review Screening Questions

☐ Evaluate Skills Assessment

☐ Round one interview

☐ Round two interview

☐ Check references

☐ Offer position

☐ Onboarding

☐ Close or remove job posting

☐ Follow up evaluation and raise if applicable

Download the Hiring
Process Toolbox at
TheJoyOfPursuit.com/Hiring

- The Hiring Process Checklist
- Team Capacity Check
- Job Description Example
- Applicant Tracking Sheet
- Screening Questions
- Skills Assessment
- Interview ScoreCARD
- What NOT to Ask in an Interview
- Interview Agenda and Questions
- Reference Check
- Onboarding Checklist

Acknowledgments

Thank you, God, for our grace-given gifts and for connecting our hearts to write this series and co-found Joy of Pursuit.

Thank you to all the candidates we have interviewed in the past. Each experience has taught us valuable lessons that are interwoven into this book.

To our families and children, thank you for your support, encouragement, and for contributing to the joy in our lives.

Amanda is known both personally and professionally for her consistency, clarity, and commitment. Her grace-given gifts of practicality and focus allow her to keep an accurate perspective in life and business. She is level-headed and gives attention to the necessary priorities without distractions slowing her down. Amanda is an action-taker with a well-thought-out plan of attack in hand.

Throughout her work history, Amanda has frequently been known as the most dependable team member. She began her career with numbers and finances but grew to discover a passion for the people-side of business in Human Resources. She has a talent for identifying uniqueness in others, encouraging them to know their worth and abilities, all while gracefully holding them accountable for their actions.

Despite years of working for a publishing company, Amanda never thought she would be an author. She is now a four-time published author with an entire series for small businesses. *The Team Solution Series: HR Coaching to Grow Teams and Profit* provides more than ideas—the books are full implementation plans to guide you and your team through the employee journey. The content blends Amanda's unparalleled organizational skills with her knowledge of HR practices. Her exceptional ability to improve efficiency and processes in organizations will serve countless small business owners and strengthen their teams.

Throughout the writing and publishing process of *The Team Solution Series* (and thanks to being business partners with a top-notch book coach), Amanda knows that if she can write a book, anyone can. Together with her business partner, Brenda Haire, they created the Author Business Network, providing authors with the tools needed to successfully write, publish, market, and build a business around their books.

Amanda and her two children live at the foothills of the Smoky Mountains in Tennessee. She enjoys hiking with her kids, cooking, and gardening, especially cultivating flowers. She's known for having some of the most beautiful blooms in town. One of the greatest joys of her life is watching her children grow and guiding them to pursue their passions.

Connect with Amanda
LinkedIn.com/in/AmandaJPainter

Brenda's had over forty jobs and has been working since she was twelve. She's never been fired and is not ashamed of her work history. Brenda always worked her way up, out, and on to the next adventure. Many see this as risky and call her fearless. She would tell you that fear was always a factor—she just chose faith instead.

After being told she was a nobody by a publisher, Brenda struggled with her identity as a writer. Not one to give up, she pursued her dream and released her first book, *Save the Butter Tubs!: Discover Your Worth in a Disposable World*, in 2018.

Brenda was immediately hired by her publishing agency after her book was released, and she went on to become the president of the company. An entrepreneur at heart, once again she left on top and now uses her experience to serve individuals and small businesses around the world as the CEO and cofounder of Joy of Pursuit. Brenda created the Author Business Network with her business partner,

Amanda Painter, and together they help authors build businesses around their books.

As a speaker, Brenda shares keynotes and workshops that transform audiences. Whether she is speaking about purpose, publishing, or small business, her deepest desire is to help you shine your light by operating in your grace-given gifts. She considers herself a moved soul—so moved by her encounters with God that she can't help but move in response. She wants the same for you—to encounter God in a way that you can't help but live a life worthy of your calling.

She and her hubs (as she lovingly refers to him on social media), Darren, are both military veterans. They enjoy hiking and chasing waterfalls across the United States and live in Texas with their beautifully blended and expanding family.

Connect with Brenda
Facebook.com/BrendaHaire
Instagram.com/BrendaAHaire
LinkedIn.com/in/Brenda Haire

Empower Your Team
Elevate Your Business

» Strategies to Find and Keep Top Talent.

» Techniques that Boost Employee Engagement and Reduce Turnover.

» Tools to Ensure Smooth Transitions and Protect Your Business.

Unlock the Full Potential
of Your Team »ENROLL NOW

TheJoyofPursuit.com/HR-Course

Revolutionize Your Business
with Our HR Consulting Services

**Executive
Consultant**

**Amanda
J. Painter**

Tailored Solutions for
Your HR Challenges

》 Streamline Processes
》 Boost Productivity
》 Reduce Costs

Start Today!
TheJoyOfPursuit.com/
store/p/HRconsult

Receive Exclusive HR Insights, Industry News, and Best Practices Straight to Your Inbox.

One email per month to take you and your business from tired and busy to thriving and productive!

Try it today

Tools.TheJoyOfPursuit.com/CutTheChaos

Take the next step in
creating a culture of growth
and fulfillment of purpose.

COMPLETE THE
TEAM SOLUTION SERIES

TheJoyOfPursuit.com/Books

Transform Your Workplace

Build a Custom Workshop for Your Team

Higher Productivity
Efficient Meetings
Lower Turnover
Engaged Employees
Cohesive Leadership Team

It's Time to Create a
Joyful Workplace
for YOU and Your Team!

TheJoyOfPursuit.com/Workshops

Buy in Bulk

for Your Human Resource Team, Directors, or Leadership Team

TheJoyofPursuit.com/Books

49234595R00091